MORE THAN
pretty

**7 Beauty Secrets
That Could Change
Your Life**

Lataya B. Simpson

MORE THAN PRETTY: 7 Beauty Secrets That Could Change Your Life
© 2013 By Lataya Simpson
All rights reserved.
ISBN-10: 0615925383
ISBN-13: 978-0615925387

No part of this publication may be reproduced, distributed, or transmitted in any form or by any means, including photocopying, recording, or other electronic or mechanical methods, without the prior written permission of the publisher, except in the case of brief quotations embodied in critical reviews and certain other noncommercial uses permitted by copyright law.
For permission requests, write to the author:

MTP Works
Attention: MORE THAN PRETTY
PO Box 722413
Houston, TX 77272

Scriptures indicated as NRSV are taken from the New Revised Standard Version Bible, copyright © 1989 the Division of Christian Education of the National Council of the Churches of Christ in the United States of America. Used by permission. All rights reserved.

Ordering Information:
Discounts are available on high volume orders. For details, contact the publisher at the address above or visit
www.latayasimpson.com

Printed in the United States of America
First Edition

Contents

Introduction 8

1. The Parable 13
2. Drawing Meaning 25
3. The Secret To Inner Beauty 35
4. Self-image 41
5. Morals & Spirituality 49
6. Work Ethic 57
7. How I Treat My Body 63
8. How I Treat My Mind 69
9. How I Treat Others 79
10. How I Treat Others (Part 2) 85
11. How I Allow Others To Treat Me 91
12. Keeping The Secret 99

References 118

...Whatever is true, whatever is honorable,
whatever is just, whatever is pure,
whatever is pleasing,
whatever is commendable,
if there is any excellence and
if there is anything worthy of praise,
think about these things.

Phil 4:8 (NRSV)

Acknowledgements

I both acknowledge and thank the Lord God for the gift of creativity, the ability to write and the opportunity to do something that will help others.

My husband, Johnnie, who loves me and believes in me, encourages me in every idea I have. I couldn't have asked for a better husband, confidant and cheerleader (yes, I called you a cheerleader).

My mother, Linda, has always believed that I could and should write a book. Thank you for believing in me; for encouraging me and never losing faith that I could do it. Thank you, Mom, for your constant love and support.

I must acknowledge my father, Dave, for challenging supporting and engaging me, stretching my thinking and always offering encouragement. I thank and acknowledge my brother, Dave, who reminds me to stay up to date. Thank you Dave for also reminding me that anything can be a business if you keep it business; thank you for that big brother.

My mother in law, LaTayne, helped inspire me to gain the momentum to write and be motivated to finish! My aunt Connie showed me that publishing is feasible.

I both acknowledge and thank my extended family and friends for a multitude of support and love.

Thank God for my children; they inspire me to share with the world the lessons I teach and learn from them.

I acknowledge Kristi, Quiana, LaFaith, Nicole, Enola, Tara and my many girlfriends who have shared life experiences, each with grace and beauty, reminding me that to be victorious in any area of life you have to be more than pretty.

Thank you to my readers and editors: Jessica, Nicole, Linda, Enola and Keidra.

And last but not least... for buying this book and reading it – thank *you* from the bottom of my heart! -LBS

Prelude

Introduction

THE SECRET TO BEING MORE THAN PRETTY...

People love hearing and telling secrets! CEOs and business owners share secrets to success. Experts write books on *The Secret to a Happy* this or that. Many great cooks have a secret ingredient to their best dishes, passed down throughout the family. In our personal lives, there is usually a family secret or two in every family that has been told more than kept.

I think the most commonly found secrets, though, are in nearly every magazine targeted at women (or men for that matter). Look on the magazine shelves and you'll find *beauty secrets* to help you improve your personal appearance in one way or another.

Beauty is a powerful force. It infiltrates nearly every area of life from a very early age. We worry about how we look when we wake up, when we go to work, church, school, shopping, and even the hospital. We crave those beauty secrets that help us be as pretty we can be.

Yet, most of us learn somewhere along the way in life that being pretty alone doesn't get you very far. Even in areas where it seems that beauty is the focus, being pretty alone only gets you through the door.

You have to be *more than pretty* to be successful in life. So what's the secret to being *more than pretty*? Let's discover the answer together starting with *The Parable of the Woman with Two Trees*...

...Where your treasure is, there your heart will be also.

Matthew 6:21 (NRSV)

THE PARABLE OF THE WOMAN WITH TWO TREES

One day, a woman decided to plant two trees, a magnolia and a maple. She planted the magnolia tree in the front yard for beauty, and the maple tree in the back yard for shade.

As the two trees grew, the woman maintained the magnolia tree very well because it was out front and visible. The maple she rarely tended because it was not seen, being in the back yard. She nurtured and cared for the tree near her front door because it was the first thing people saw when coming to visit or passing by her home.

Many years passed, and both trees grew tall. The woman focused the majority of her attention on this beautiful magnolia tree. As a result it grew strong and beautiful and many people told her how lovely the tree looked in her yard.

She purchased different products suggested by a tree specialist to make sure that the magnolia tree looked healthy and vibrant. She did everything she could to make sure that the tree out front always looked great.

As for the maple tree out back, it just grew tall and wild. It was unseen, being out back, so she didn't see the point in investing time and money into it. Instead of hiring a specialist to examine and trim the tree, she just did it herself. Because she wasn't an expert, she didn't know how hazardous the tree had become because it had not been properly pruned and trimmed.

One day there was a hurricane; it was strong and fierce. The strong winds blew hard and the rain poured down as if from buckets! People were instructed to evacuate the area, which the woman did, because the storm was so frightening and overwhelming.

Throughout the neighborhood many homes were damaged as a result of the storm. Trees were uprooted; some had broken trunks, some split. Yet, at the woman's home, the magnolia tree out front stood beautifully in the midst of the wind and rain.

Its branches bent but didn't break. It stood strong because it had been consistently and properly pruned and cared for over the years. It was beautiful before the storm and it was beautiful after the storm.

In the backyard however, the maple tree, which had not been well cared for, did not fare so well. When the hurricane was over, many of the tree's wild and overgrown branches were broken and had blown away. Thankfully, the trunk of the maple tree had not broken or split. The tree survived but was a mess after enduring the weight of the storm.

After the hurricane, the woman returned to see how her home fared. She surveyed the front yard, disappointed that her perfect garden around her perfect magnolia tree was trampled by the wind. She carefully examined her front yard tree, making sure it was in good shape and looked beautiful.

She was proud that her tree had stood well against the storm, surviving the wind's abuse. She decided to use a string of decorative lights to make the tree look better while she got her garden back in shape. As she was making her plans, she decided to see how the rest of her property had fared. She was devastated by what she discovered.

The woman's home was now damaged because the long wild tree had crashed through the roof, causing her home to be flooded with rain water. Her back yard was in shambles. Long, big, heavy branches were strewn all over her yard and even hanging over the fence. The maple tree was in bad shape and had left everything around it in chaos. Even nearby homes and power lines were damaged by her tree. The woman couldn't believe her eyes.

Although it was recommended that everyone evacuate the area, some of the woman's neighbors had stayed home. During her investigation into the damage, she learned that a close neighbor who had stayed home was injured when the overgrown branches from her tree blew through his window.

She was mortified! The woman never expected anything like this, especially after seeing how well the tree out front had lasted. That night, the woman cried in great sorrow, thinking about how many more people that could have been hurt as a result of this tree that she had not cared for. She was embarrassed, angry, hurt, and ashamed of what she had allowed to happen by not taking care of this tree in her back yard. All those years she thought the maple tree didn't matter because it was in her back yard and no one would ever see it. Unfortunately, she had been wrong.

The tree in the back mattered even more than the one in the front because it affected more people, being closer to many neighbors. Now someone was hurt as a result of her not caring for the unseen tree. She wondered how much it would cost to repair the damage that she had inadvertently caused by not taking care of this unseen tree.

At some point she got angry at the *storm* because in her mind, if it had not been for the *storm*, this wouldn't have happened. It didn't take long for her to realize that the damage was her fault and responsibility.

That same night, she made a promise to herself that she would do everything she could to make things right, even if that meant getting help. This woman reached out to all of her neighbors and made efforts to help them remedy their situations. She helped them clean up the broken branches her tree had lost in their yards. She offered to help pay for the damaged rooftops and broken windows. She also apologized sincerely, regretting being irresponsible in maintaining the unseen tree.

Some accepted her apologies; some did not. Some accepted her help. Some rejected her because of the devastation she had inadvertently caused during this storm. Though all those years she thought the tree was unseen, they all saw that the tree was dangerous before the storm and had tried to tell her to get help with it.

She considered cutting the tree down, but couldn't. The roots were too intricately woven under her home from the years of growth. The woman called a tree care specialist to come examine her maple tree and see if it could be salvaged, as well as a foundation repair specialist and roofing company to see if her home could be repaired.

It took a lot of time, money, work and patience to get her home back in shape.

Meanwhile, the beautiful, perfectly pruned, perfectly decorated tree out front had become less important. As time passed, she carefully maintained the tree in the back, called the specialist for a regular exam and kept the newly grown branches properly trimmed. She didn't neglect the tree out front; she just spent less time worrying about making sure it always looked perfect.

> *The woman realized that it was just as important to invest time, energy and money in caring for the unseen as it was to care for something that is seen by everyone passing by.*

When the next storm came, both trees stood strong. Both trees had been well cared for, with the help of a professional. With continuous care both would last a very long time.

*It's more than a story...
it's the reality of our lives*

Drawing Meaning

A lot of meaning can be drawn from *The Parable of the Woman with Two Trees*. When it was written, the intention was to demonstrate the value of personal development. It was also written to demonstrate the potential negative effects of focusing more on the outer appearance than our inner being.

To better understand it, let's look at all of the characters and story elements:

The Woman

The woman in this story represents you, me and every person.

The Magnolia Tree

The magnolia tree represents our outer appearance, hair, nails, face, clothes, accessories, social status, etc.

The Maple Tree

The maple tree represents the inner being... the spirit, heart, mind, emotional wellbeing and coping abilities.

The garden and decorative lights around the magnolia

These elements represent all the additional and unnecessary accessories we use to complement our beauty and hide our flaws. We spend time and money on things to make us look good... but how much do these things really matter?

THE STORMS

The storms represent crisis, tragedy, the trials of life, and general ups and downs. When a person is in a crisis, lashing out in a way that could hurt others can often happen, sometimes unintentionally. Let's look at the neighbors to see what I mean.

THE NEIGHBORS

The neighbors represent the people (family, friends and strangers) who are affected by our rhetorical unkempt maple tree.

People get hurt when we don't manage stress well. For example, being unkind or aggressive because you're angry, exhibiting road rage due to stress, giving bad advice based on bitterness from past hurts, offering a discouraging word because you're discouraged; these are all ways people can be hurt when we don't take care of our inner being. We sometimes unintentionally make the old adage, "misery loves company," come true at our own hands.

The Woman's Home

The woman's home represents physical wellbeing. Just as the unkempt tree damaged the foundation of the home, if we aren't careful, our emotions will contribute to major damage in our bodies. Our health is affected by our emotional ups and downs.

Coping poorly with stress will take its toll on your body. In fact, stress is one of the causes for all kinds of illnesses such as headaches, heart disease, asthma, gastrointestinal problems and even Alzheimer's[i].

THE TREE CARE SPECIALIST

This character represents professional help such as psychologists, spiritual advisors, coaches and other individuals or groups that can help us cope with life's issues on a professional level. Often, we try to fix ourselves, but talking to a counselor or a professional of some sort can be quite beneficial and even necessary. This is true because in many cases we don't know how to dig deeper to get to the root of our problem(s).

THE FOUNDATION REPAIR SPECIALIST AND ROOFING COMPANY

These represent medical doctors.
Previously, I mentioned that stress is a leading cause of many diseases. If left

untreated, many of the diseases caused by stress can make you miserable or even take your life. While stress isn't the only cause of heart disease, obesity, headaches, and asthma (along with a host of other ailments), it can't be stressed enough that neglecting your inner being can wreak havoc on your outer being. Having a pretty face in a casket will do you no good if your life comes to an end too soon as a result of a heart attack or stroke.

Observation

The Parable of the Woman with Two Trees is a great example of a very sad observation: The average woman spends more time, money and energy on personal appearance than on her own personal development. This is not a statistic that I can attribute to a specific study. This is simply an observation.

Hair, makeup, nails, clothes and accessories all take up a great amount of time and money to maintain. Social status can play a part in that as well. As women, we think about things that will help us look better, we read about these things, we talk about these things. We even set regular appointments at salons to make sure we look our best.

The media and beauty industry reinforces the need to spend time, energy and money on personal appearance. They endorse new

> *We should ask ourselves, why are we as a culture willing to invest so much into personal appearance?*

beauty secrets on television, in magazines, online and even on our phones through ads and text messages. In general, we as a culture want the world to be a more beautiful place, starting with our own faces, bodies and lifestyles. Although beauty care makes us look good and perhaps even feel good, how important is it really?

We tell ourselves and children who are growing up that inner beauty matters the most. We talk about how important it is to have a positive self-image and high self-esteem; yet consider the amount of time spent on *teaching* young people (and the young at heart) how to develop inner beauty.

When we don't work on inner beauty (i.e., personal development) we are like the tree in the backyard that caused so much damage. We are more likely to hurt and damage the people around us and/or ourselves. It is both necessary and beneficial for each and every human being to spend time, money and energy on taking care of self.

True beauty secrets are those that help you develop into a beautiful person from the inside out!

Along With Not Instead Of

Understand that the concept of *More Than Pretty* does not suggest that we neglect outer beauty. The goal is to help us all learn to be intentional about focusing *more* on what's more important.

Chapter 3

THE SECRET TO INNER BEAUTY

Much like outer beauty, inner beauty begins with being healthy. Healthy skin, hair, teeth and nails can contribute to making a woman glow! The opposite is also true, at times; an unhealthy body may physically show some sign of that state.

With inner beauty, being healthy or unhealthy is not as obvious because this is a type of beauty that you can't always see immediately or at glance. Emotional health, not physical health, is what directly affects inner beauty and inner beauty is projected in how a person lives.

Preventive Care For Emotional Health

Doctors and experts will often recommend certain wellness methods to help prevent unhealthy outcomes.[ii] Though it is not a guarantee for perfect health, preventive care reduces the risk for certain cancers, heart disease, obesity and certain viruses; it also saves you money long term. Preventive care can also help prevent OTHERS from being negatively affected by your health issues and resulting needs such as long or short term caregiving.

Preventive care doesn't apply to physical health only. There are steps any person can take to be proactive in improving emotional wellbeing.

Psychologist Candice Mays states, "Doing things that you enjoy, surrounding yourself with positive and supportive people, getting enough sleep, and minimizing stress are all ways that people can increase the likelihood of good mental health."

Understand that there are some conditions that require medical attention or prescription drugs. Anti-depressants, anti-psychotics along with many other stimulants and steroids are sometimes necessary for maintaining certain conditions. Each person should consult a physician *and* psychologist before taking any of these medications, which should be administered by prescription only. Even with prescription drugs, every person has a responsibility to make good decisions for his or her own emotional health and wellbeing.

Emotional health directly affects our inner beauty because self-esteem, self-worth, happiness and inner peace are all elements that affect how we live, behave and interact.

"Beauty Secrets" For Personal Development

I believe that how we allow others to treat us, how we treat others, our body and mind; work ethic, morals, spirituality and self-image are some of the elements of inner beauty. Prevention is the best beauty secret around, in regard to both physical and inner beauty. It is also important to address issues that arise before they become a *problem*. It is also critical address issues that have *already* become a problem through personal development.

Personal development is a phrase that is intimidating or confusing to some. In my opinion that's primarily because most people don't know where to begin with the concept. Frankly there is not a perfect formula; every person is different with different issues. It's only through personal assessment that we can effectively invest in personal development because that's when we'll be able to see what needs to be addressed. Let's dig deeper and take a look at these elements through seven beauty secrets that could change your life, starting with self-image.

Beauty Secret #1

Choosing to have a positive self-image is a beautiful thing.

Chapter 4

SELF-IMAGE

A woman with a positive self-image will set goals because she believes that she can accomplish them. She will speak well of herself, not bragging or putting herself down publicly or privately.

She will watch her diet and exercise for her health rather than just to look good in a pair of skinny jeans ... but if looking good in *any* jeans is a byproduct of a healthy diet and exercise she probably won't complain!

A woman with a positive self-image will not be emotionally swayed by what others think of her. She will not assume the worst in others' opinions of her but has an inner peace in spite of any circumstances.

A woman with a positive self-image may *occasionally* have fleeting moments of self-doubt, but a woman with a positive self-image will recognize it and overcome that doubt with no trouble.

A woman with a positive self-image will extend grace when offended and not hold unnecessary grudges.

I would love to be this woman! I think all women would love to be this woman, but for the most part, most *people* (including me and not only women) can't say that we are successful at doing all of these things all of the time (and that's ok).

What's not ok is confusing self-image with public image. Any passerby would have assumed that the woman in the parable had a great green thumb, and took good care of all of her trees. They would have only been half-right because there was no balance. Likewise, there are lots of people in the world who have a great public image but have a distorted view of self.

Many famous people (such as entertainers, athletes, politicians and even pastors) sometimes tarnish their public image through their surprisingly negative behavior while away from their respective stages. Many of us have seen the stories of the person who made unkind remarks to a reporter. Some of us have also seen a famous person caught up in a twitter battle with a now former fan. Sadly, there are also the instances where a public figure is caught using slurs or derogatory language.

We as the public may find ourselves disappointed in these people when things like this happen. But the truth is, most of the time we don't know if those people were going through a personal crisis which may have caused them to be a bit more sensitive, testy or downright nasty. Understand that these people are not exempt from the human condition and the resulting "storms" of life.

We should extend grace rather than judgment. Remember it's hard for a public figure to escape the limelight in this, as I call it, *instant media age*. Their flaws end up on the same big screen as the talents they are known and loved for. I'm sure none of us would want our behavior displayed to the public when we are at our emotional worst.

Whether you are a public figure or a "regular Joe" or "Jane," be careful not to confuse your public image or professional image with self-image. No doubt, we are all flawed but how we respond to what happens in our lives is a choice. Those responses can also give us a glimpse into our own self-image, self-esteem and self-worth. Often we discover we are not the people we hope to be, I know that has been true for me. The good news is that working on personal development can help us all become the people we want to be.

Throughout this book, you'll discover a series of checklists that I hope you will find helpful in beginning a personal assessment. In this chapter, the checklist is derived from the opening anecdote about "a woman with a positive self-image." This gives a simple foundation on how to start in assessing and/or developing a positive self-image yourself.

Ask yourself, "How am I doing in these areas?"

- ✓ What I believe about myself
- ✓ Positive thoughts, affirmations
- ✓ Goal setting
- ✓ Speaking well of self
- ✓ Health, wellness, fitness
- ✓ Managing emotions and coping skills
- ✓ How I respond to offenses

These are some of the areas in our lives that we can assess and address in improving self-image. Other chapters will go into more detail on some of these areas. You can make a longer list to work from if you choose because developing one's self-image can't be confined to only these things.

Having a positive self-image is your choice. I believe that uncovering this beauty secret and addressing it strategically is essential for changing and improving your life.

Beauty Secret

#2

Having grounded spirituality and morals is a beautiful thing.

Morals & Spirituality

For me, morality is rooted in spirituality and my spirituality is based on my beliefs as a Christian so I will base this chapter on my personal beliefs.

The Bible, being the foundational tool for Christian believers, has many lessons on how to live in a scripturally moral way that would be pleasing to God. It also offers instruction on how to develop spiritually.

The word "morals" is defined[iii] as:

"Founded on fundamental principles of right conduct rather than on legalities."

Whether we like it or not, what is *moral* is subjective. I chose this specific definition because it highlights the idea that right conduct is not necessarily based on law.

As I stated earlier in this chapter, my morals are based on my spirituality, which is based on my faith as Christian. Our behavior should reflect what we believe to be morally acceptable. Negative behavior or that which goes against our own moral compass is like a blemish to our inner beauty.

> *Your beliefs may differ from mine but we should respect all people regardless of any difference in religious beliefs.*

There are a few things I do on a regular basis to ensure that I am making decisions that line up with my core beliefs. I pray, read the Bible, listen to uplifting messages, serve and hang out with people who have similar beliefs or as some people refer to it, I fellowship. I also get advice from people I trust when I need it.

Regardless of any difference in beliefs, these five elements of spirituality are proven to be beneficial[iv]:

- ✓ Prayer
- ✓ Reading (the Bible and other related materials such as devotionals)
- ✓ Fellowship, Making Friends
- ✓ Serving
- ✓ Good Advice /Uplifting Messages

Much like the checklist regarding self-image, this checklist can be a tool in helping you develop spiritually and enhance your inner beauty.

There is no recipe for what's enough of any of these elements. Each one of us must choose our own moral compass. For me, that moral compass is my spirituality through my relationship with God in Jesus Christ. (If you're not sure that you have a moral compass, know that now is a great time to make a choice that could change your life.)

Personally, when I don't spend enough time in prayer or reading the Bible or something related, my decision making is affected in a negative way. The opposite is also true: when I spend more time doing these things my decision making and clarity of thought is better and my life in general is better for it. I also find that I have a greater peace of mind which is a great part of inner beauty and a big step in personal development.

I've found that fellowship and serving are also great for my spiritual development as well. I combine these because for me, serving has provided me an opportunity to experience both of these simultaneously. I believe we all have gifts and talents. Everyone is good at something so we should all find a way to serve in an area where we can put our talents to good use.

Serving is a Biblical teaching[v] so as a part of my spirituality, I serve through ministry using my talent for media production and writing. As a result, I've made lifelong friends, shared my joys and heartaches with people I've met through serving in this ministry. As a result of spending time with people who have similar beliefs, I benefit from "positive peer pressure." Positive peer pressure is encouragement to make good decisions. I also had an opportunity to serve God by serving others.

Finally, good advice is a great benefit when trying to make good (and moral) decisions. Let's be honest, the right choice isn't always the first thought that comes to mind when decision making time rolls around. There are times we have ideas or opportunities that could ultimately go against our core beliefs or moral compass. Having a spiritual advisor helps keep a person grounded in faith and ultimately in better (moral) decision making.[vi]

In my experience the same is true for listening to uplifting messages in a group setting like at church, a Bible study or a retreat. I also think everyone needs to have multiple sources for advice to be sure you always get wise counsel.

I can't say one of these elements is more important than the other. I think you need to have balance in these five areas to be grounded in your spiritual life or faith.

My spiritual life is enriched greatly through these five elements which is why I consider this a life changing beauty secret. As a result of developing my inner beauty through enriching my spiritual life I become more beautiful inside which is projected more ways than we know.

Beauty Secret

#3

Choosing to have a good work ethic is a beautiful thing.

WORK ETHIC

Whether we realize it or not, work ethic contributes to inner beauty. When we feel good (or bad) about work performance, that feeling can spill over into how we interact with others. With or without a job, everyone has an opportunity to exercise work ethic.

Be it in the workplace, your community or at home, it's important to start and finish projects with good work ethic, do them well and to your satisfaction. I remind myself of the woman in the parable. There are some things that I take care of really well and others that I forget or unintentionally neglect. How about you?

I will confess that I, personally, have a hard time finishing household chores. Even as you read this book, I probably have a couple loads of laundry and dishes that need to be loaded into or out of their respective washers. (It's embarrassing and I don't like it... but it's true.)

In spite of this, every day I work on household chores, whether I can keep up or catch up. I will never stop working on it, not to prove something to myself or anyone else but because, frankly, the need won't go away. While this isn't satisfactory for me, I don't quit. The point is, even if you're not the best, or even if you feel you aren't doing your best, don't quit. If the work is your responsibility keep working at getting better and keep working at getting the job done well and to your personal satisfaction.

Personally, I had to hire a professional organizer along with asking family and to come help me at home. I realized I wasn't capable of managing it all on my own. Who is your "tree specialist" when you have a problem? This coach was mine.

As a part of your personal development, here is another checklist to utilize that may help you grow, improve or evaluate your work ethic:

- ✓ Accomplishments, Achievements
- ✓ Failures, Incomplete projects
- ✓ Weak or challenging areas
- ✓ Where I (can) get help

Observing what I've accomplished (and how I did it) has helped me see that I have a very strong work ethic. There are areas, however, where I need to improve or get help on so that my work ethic will be more balanced and consistent in different areas of my life. Seeing my accomplishments inspires and motivates me to be able to do better in the areas where I need to improve. Maybe it will do the same for you.

This beauty secret is life changing because a poor work ethic or being out of balance can be detrimental. The woman in the story had a great work ethic when it came to caring for her tree in the front yard. However, her work ethic was terrible when it came to the tree in the back yard. As a result people were hurt.

What qualities do you see in yourself in regard to work ethic? Do you feel that you have a strong work ethic? Is your work ethic balanced or do you find yourself missing the mark consistently in certain areas? Is it possibly causing you to interact negatively with others?

Self-assessment is the first step in taking good care of yourself so that you can be the best that you can be. I encourage you to embrace this step in your personal development.

Remember, self-assessment is a beauty secret that only works when it leads to self-improvement. Assessment is only the beginning of proper treatment when it comes to physical, mental or emotional health. Remember that this is a good way to take care of you.

Beauty Secret

#4

Treating your body well
is a beautiful thing.

Chapter 7

How I Treat My Body

One of the teachings in the Bible is that your body is "a temple." I believe this means your body should be treated with honor and respect. I can't tell anyone how to live, but I can encourage and challenge you to assess how you treat your body.

Ask yourself, "Do I show my body respect? Do my habits relating to dietary habits, exercise, sleep, drugs, alcohol, environment and exposure reflect those of a person who respects his or her body?"

Here is a checklist to help guide you and help you assess your habits toward your body:

- ✓ Exercise
- ✓ Dietary habits
- ✓ Drugs, alcohol
- ✓ Abuse (self-inflicted or by another individual)
- ✓ Checkups at the doctor, dentist etc.
- ✓ Sleep
- ✓ Does the way I dress reflect my self-respect and inner beauty?

Anything unhealthy needs to be addressed and eliminated. I do recognize that statements like that are a lot easier said than done. My suggestion is that you start with an easily executable idea like going to the doctor for a check-up or physical. Next, incorporate taking a walk once or twice a week and maybe build up to working out on a regular basis. Maybe cut back on fried foods or sweets. Try cutting back on alcohol or nicotine. Whatever you decide to do is up to you; just make actionable steps toward treating your body in a way that you can respect.

> *Assessment is the first step in taking good care of you.*

In *The Parable of the Woman with Two Trees*, the woman inadvertently neglected her "body" which was represented by the home, by not recognizing the damage that the maple tree was causing.

When my blood pressure is increasing or I begin gaining weight, I have to ask myself is there something emotional that I should be dealing with that is causing my body to respond? I encourage you to do the same and if you find that the answer is yes don't wait to address it.

Lastly, it seems that fashion and styles change with every season and as times changes, what's acceptable in the way we dress has changed as well. Regardless of the current trends, be confident in your attire by occasionally ask yourself, "If I could communicate my level of self-respect and display my inner beauty by the way I dress, is this ensemble the best choice?"

Remember, just as it is important not to confuse your public image with your self-image, it is also important to never let your public image affect your self-image. Be conscious about not allowing your style and attire to distract you or others from the person you are on the inside.

Here's another beauty secret: self-respect is an attribute of inner beauty; it can't be measured but it can be intentional. Be intentional about showing yourself respect through how you treat your body.

Beauty Secret

#5

Treating your mind well

is a beautiful thing.

How I Treat My Mind

I have always been a strong proponent of education. Formal education isn't for everyone but that doesn't put any limitations on learning. Libraries are filled with books that can be checked out; the internet is loaded with tons of useful information and lots of organizations host classes on a variety of subjects.

With or without formal education, it's important to feed your mind well because whether intentional or not, we're always learning and thinking. Having healthy thoughts is a choice.

Remember *The Parable of the Woman with Two Trees;* your mind is like the "maple tree" in your backyard. If you neglect it, others are affected. Here's how: Think of all of the things you could accomplish if you knew how to do more. Think of all the causes you could support if you knew more about certain issues. Think of all of the money you could make (or save) if you knew more and as a result use that money to send your children to college, take care of aging parents, or give to a charity.

What we do with our minds has the potential to affect our own lives as well as the entire world tremendously. Feed your mind with positive images and get educated on those things that you're passionate about. You will be amazed at what you will be able to accomplish, the lives that will be changed and the people you will inspire when you treat your mind well.

Part of treating your mind well includes pruning away dead thoughts and producing "fruit" by actively sharing what you've learned.

Your Mind and Your Passion

Do you know what you're passionate about? It may seem like a silly question to some, but for most of us, what we passionately *pursue* isn't actually what we are passionate *about*. The old saying, "You can't see the forest for the trees," comes to mind when I think of this idea.

There was a time in my life where I would volunteer extensively for an organization because I was passionate about what we were doing and passionate about service. However, because of the many tasks that had to be accomplished, I found very little time to actually do the specific thing that I was passionate about.

In the meantime my car was about to be repossessed because I didn't have steady income. I was so focused on the little tasks that I didn't realize that I wasn't allowing myself time to look for a job that would afford me the opportunity to serve while making an income.

When I realized what happened, I found a way to serve the community while employed in a similar role. I revisited the very thing I had been doing as a volunteer and I was able more effectively focus on what I was passionate about without so many distractions. I could now see the *forest* and the *trees*. When I wasn't bogged down with so many tasks I was able to learn more about what I was passionate about and become more effective in my performance of it.

In terms of how you treat your mind, I believe it's important to discover what you're passionate about so that as you learn, you're actively and intentionally

> Thomas Edison once said, "If we did all the things we are capable of, we would literally astonish ourselves." That kind of astonishment starts with feeding your mind the right way.

learning about those things that will help you pursue your passion effectively.

Here is a checklist to help you assess yourself and get your mind and thoughts in shape for that which you are passionate about:

- ✓ Write down why (why am I passionate about this?)
- ✓ Discover through articles, books, videos and classes
- ✓ Share ideas and talk to others
- ✓ Set & reach related goals
- ✓ Be honest (with self & with others regarding your abilities and passion)
- ✓ Positive thinking
- ✓ Positive surroundings

No one can see what's in your mind, sometimes not even you. It's a common myth that we as human beings only use

10% of our mental capacity. However, we should all ask ourselves, "Am I using my mental capacity to my greatest benefit?"

If you find it hard to clarify what you're passionate about, think back to 5, 10 or 20 years ago to what got you excited or made you angry. Think back on those things that made you exceedingly happy or sad. Then ask yourself why these things made you feel that way. Now ask yourself if those things are still important to you and if not, what makes you excited, happy, angry or sad now.

You can rediscover your passion or develop a new passion if you take the time to get to know YOU. As a result of this kind of personal development, your inner beauty will shine through in your actions, character and disposition.

This beauty secret may be the most valuable in my opinion because if your mind isn't well cared for then you can't master any of the other secrets.

The Everyday Beauty Competition

There is a distinct difference between being *more than pretty* and prettier than average. "Pretty" is subjective, what I think is beautiful may not be beautiful to the next person and what you think is beautiful may be ugly to another. This means "pretty" should have no power.

This is an important concept because all too often we participate in an "everyday beauty competition." Often favoritism is shown to those who appear to be prettier than average in the eye of the beholder. Unfortunately this can lead to inflated egos and false confidence. Often hurt feelings and damaged self-esteem are the result for those who are not shown the same generosity, kindness or grace.

No matter who you are, I dare you to give no power to "pretty" because at the end of the day, there is so much more to life than being pretty.

Beauty Secret #6

Treating others well is a beautiful thing.

How I Treat Others

If you went to public school in the US, you probably learned a few common sayings. The Golden Rule: Do unto others as you would have them do unto you[vii]. Another famous line from most of our childhoods: If you can't say anything nice, don't say anything at all. And finally: sticks and stones may break my bones but words will never hurt me.

Well... along the way the Golden Rule has definitely been broken. And many people hide behind the idea of "telling the truth" to get away with being unkind. We know that words hurt as badly as sticks and stones, in some cases worse because these are wounds that often go untreated.

While secret No. 5 may be most important, how a person treats others, in my opinion, is the single most common way we as decide or judge if someone is as beautiful "on the inside" as they are on the outside.

For example, often how a man or a woman treats the waiter on the first date determines whether or not there is a future in the relationship. How a model treats a photographer, how a student treats other students, how a salesperson treats the receptionist are also all great examples of tests to our inner beauty.

This beauty secret is so important because it takes more than looking and sounding good on the outside to get through life successfully (and that's in community, business, family and love). As we interact with others, how pretty we are doesn't matter if we do or don't treat people well.

Looking at your life, ask yourself:

- ✓ Am I honest with people?
- ✓ Do I keep or break promises?
- ✓ Do I treat people equally *and* fairly?
- ✓ Am I biased or unbiased toward certain people?
- ✓ Am I kind or unkind?
- ✓ Do I assert power in a fair or unfair way?

No one is perfect, not one of us. Very few people in the world will be able to get all of the answers to these questions right all of the time. Just as with every other area, this is a simple checklist to help you assess yourself, your behavior and your attitude so that you can make improvements or help others in the areas where you are strong.

In *The Parable of the Woman with Two Trees,* the weak maple tree damaged so many homes during the storm. Similarly, often when people go through trials or storms in life, others get hurt or damaged in the process. Unfortunately the person going through the storm usually doesn't recognize that his or her behavior is unhealthy and harmful.

Know that developing into a healthy "maple tree" doesn't happen overnight, it takes continuous care. Family, friends and strangers do not deserve to be casualties of any person's neglect of their inner wellbeing.

Follow the Golden Rule, but the secret to accomplishing this is to first treat yourself well so that you can treat others well too.

Dependents

How I Treat Others
(Part 2)

In *The Parable of the Woman with Two Trees*, the neighbors were hurt because of the woman's neglect of the back yard tree, which represents a lack of emotional self-care. Those neighbors represent the people in our lives who are affected or hurt by our words and actions. It is easy to look at this parable and carefully consider, "How do I treat my coworkers, friends, siblings?" However, I want to challenge you to ask yourself, "How do I treat those who depend on me?"

First let's talk about children. If we have them in our lives, these little people are often the first victims to our unaddressed issues when we are going through a storm, big or small. Adults often lose patience, communicate ineffectively, and set unreasonable expectations along with many other things when feeling stressed or tired.

> *Communicating ineffectively can include yelling or not speaking loud enough, refusing to repeat a directive/request or being inconsistent.*

I want to challenge you, just as I challenge myself, to teach kids how to cope with stress by how you behave when you are dealing with stress yourself. Your inner beauty is critical when dealing with kids because we help shape them into the beautiful creatures they grow up to be.

For example, when my children are having extreme upsets I tell them to count. They love counting and it can calm them down. Now they know that when they need to calm down, they should count. What's really exciting is that I now remember to count when I'm feeling stressed too now!

Next, let's talk about the elderly. In most cases, elderly people require a little more patience, kindness, respect and care. Some elderly people lose the ability to care for themselves, which can feel devastating, humiliating and shameful. It is important to always treat all people with consideration, kindness and respect, but especially the elderly and those who cannot take care of themselves.

Be sensitive to the elderly people that you care for or encounter and their need for significance and respect. It is a need we all have, regardless of age. Even in cases where the person seems to be less lucid than they were in their younger days, humiliation is still a very real emotion when a person *feels* dishonored.

Do you treat elderly with honor and respect at *all* times? Be completely honest with yourself in this. Then challenge yourself to be as considerate and sensitive toward the elderly in your words, actions *and* thoughts as you would want someone to be toward you in a position of need as you mature in age.

Neither age nor position forces anyone to relinquish his or her own dignity.

Beauty Secret

#7

Recognizing how you allow others to treat you is a beautiful thing.

How I Allow Others To Treat Me

In my opinion, there is a huge misunderstanding in the world which is: respect is earned, not given. Though this statement sounds good, respect can't be earned. Respect can only be shown.

Every person by virtue of being born deserves to be shown respect. How we demand for it to be shown to us is each person's choice.

How do you allow others to treat you? Do you allow people to put you on a pedestal, being treated with more honor or esteem than necessary? Or on the contrary, do you allow others to treat you like a modern day Cinderella without the glass slippers? Are there people who are afraid of or intimidated by you? Are you being abused emotionally, verbally or physically? What kind of behavior or treatment do you encourage when it comes to how people treat you?

Paying attention to how people treat you early on in any relationship can help you anticipate and hopefully prevent what could potentially be an unhealthy outcome. Maybe you need to have a hard conversation with a loved one or your manager; maybe you need to walk away from a hurtful or dangerous relationship; or perhaps you need to be more open and when it comes to dealing with people who feel intimidated by you.

> There are times in life when we have no control over how a person treats us. Those times include childhood, when you're in a dangerous situation, when you are in a place of total submission and when you are fully and completely dependent on someone else physically. If this isn't the case, remember you have a choice to walk away.

Like the lists in the previous chapters, the checklist in this chapter is not exhaustive. It is simply a starting place to help you assess your life in this area so that you can see where you may need to make some changes.

I encourage you to be completely honest with yourself in answering each of these questions:

- ✓ Does anyone fear me? Why?
- ✓ Do I fear anyone? Why?
- ✓ Have I been manipulated?
- ✓ Have I been abused physically?
- ✓ Have I been abused verbally?
- ✓ Am I shown respect and courtesy?

This list should be applied to your home life, social life and professional life. Some people are treated like royalty at home but like second class citizens in the workplace. Then there are those who are treated like a super hero in the community and social circles but like a super villain at home. The parallels could go on and on but I hope you get my point.

How you allow others to treat you is a critical part of personal development because it can affect your self-esteem and self-worth. If you find that you don't like the way you are being treated, do something about it. By doing so, you could prevent a lifetime of unnecessary pain for yourself and/or the people around you.

It is often said that people who have been hurt are a part of a cycle of pain because they hurt other people. Break the cycle by paying attention to how others treat you. It may be that you are unintentionally being abusive or unwittingly being abused somehow.

By taking time to recognize how you allow others to treat you, you implement a beauty secret that could not only change your life but possibly even save your life.

Never allow your perception of beauty to negatively affect how you allow others treat you.

Conclusion

KEEPING THE SECRET

Have you heard the story of how precious metals like gold and silver are purified? A goldsmith or a silversmith will place the metal into the hottest part of the fire until the heat causes all of the impurities to rise to the surface. However this is only done so that those impurities can be removed.

Unlike fire in regards to metals, the storms that come in our lives are not for the sole purpose of removing flaws. In spite of this, I encourage you to *use* your storms, much like a silversmith uses fire, to improve yourself and address any "impurities" (i.e. character flaws). Take advantage of every opportunity for personal assessment, growth and improvement. Take advantage of this book to begin to address your issues before they become a problem and cause others to be hurt if they haven't already.

Life is full of ups and downs and like the parable, there will be times where storms will come and go, as we all know. Remember, the tree in the front yard made it through the storm unscathed because it had been well cared for (through preventive care) while the tree in the back yard was nearly destroyed under the pressure of the storm. If the maple tree had been as well tended as the magnolia tree, it would have likely stood strong and produced fewer casualties!

I hope you noticed that not one of the seven profound beauty secrets found in this book was exclusive, elusive or difficult to achieve. You can accomplish each one.

Focus on keeping the greatest beauty secret there is (which is personal development) close to your heart. As you grow, I know that your beauty will shine from the inside out. You won't become perfect, but hopefully, if it is your desire, you'll be able to cope with life a little bit better. Work on the inner you! When you do I am confident that you will see, along with the rest of the world, that you truly are *more than pretty*!

Did *More Than Pretty* make an impact on you? If so, I want to hear from you!

Visit www.latayasimpson.com and look for *More Than Pretty* to share your feedback or your story.

Checklists

Did you find the checklists included in this book helpful? Each list has been extracted on the following pages for your convenience.

Honestly ask yourself, "Do I need to improve in any of these areas?

SELF-IMAGE

- ✓ What I believe about myself
- ✓ Positive thoughts, affirmations
- ✓ Goal setting
- ✓ Speaking well of self
- ✓ Health, wellness, fitness
- ✓ Managing emotions and coping skills
- ✓ How I respond to offenses

MORALS & SPIRITUALITY

- ✓ Prayer
- ✓ Reading (the Bible and other related materials such as devotionals)
- ✓ Fellowship, Making Friends
- ✓ Serving
- ✓ Good Advice /Uplifting Messages

WORK ETHIC

- ✓ Accomplishments, Achievements
- ✓ Failures, Incomplete projects
- ✓ Weak or challenging areas
- ✓ Where I (can) get help

HOW I TREAT MY BODY

- ✓ Dietary habits
- ✓ Drugs, alcohol
- ✓ Abuse (self-inflicted or by others)
- ✓ Medical Checkups
- ✓ Sleep
- ✓ Does the way I dress reflect my self-respect and inner beauty?

HOW I TREAT MY MIND

- ✓ Write down why (why am I passionate about this?)
- ✓ Discover through articles, books, videos and classes
- ✓ Share ideas and talk to others
- ✓ Set & reach related goals
- ✓ Be honest (with self, with others regarding abilities and passion)
- ✓ Positive thinking
- ✓ Positive surroundings

HOW I TREAT OTHERS

- ✓ Am I honest with people?
- ✓ Do I keep or break promises?
- ✓ Do I treat people equally AND fairly?
- ✓ Am I biased or unbiased toward certain people?
- ✓ Am I kind or am I unkind?
- ✓ Do I assert power in a fair or unfair way?

HOW I ALLOW OTHERS TO TREAT ME

- ✓ Does anyone fear me? Why?
- ✓ Do I fear anyone? Why?
- ✓ Have I been manipulated?
- ✓ Have I been abused physically?
- ✓ Have I been abused verbally?
- ✓ Am I shown respect?

REFERENCES

---

[i] The information regarding the stress related illnesses can be found on WebMD via this link
http://www.webmd.com/balance/stress-management/features/10-fixable-stress-related-health-problems

[ii] Look online at the Centers for Disease Control and Prevention web site http://www.cdc.gov/

[iii] Definition of MORALS
http://dictionary.reference.com/browse/morals?s=t

[iv] Supporting data for morals and spirituality
Prayer: http://www.webmd.com/balance/guide/prayer-topic-overview

Reading http://healthylifecarenews.com/five-health-benefits-of-reading-books/

Fellowship http://www.webmd.com/balance/features/good-friends-are-good-for-you

Serving
http://www.webmd.com/heart/news/20130614/volunteering-may-be-good-for-the-heart-in-more-ways-than-one

[v] **Bible reference**
http://www.biblegateway.com/passage/?search=1%20peter%204:10&version=NRSV

[vi] **Bible Reference**
http://www.biblegateway.com/passage/?search=psalm%201&version=NRSV

[vii] The Golden Rule is actually another quote from the Bible:
http://www.biblegateway.com/passage/?search=matthew%207:12&version=NRSV

About the Author

Lataya B. Simpson wrote *More Than Pretty* during her own journey of personal development. Her goal is to inspire each reader to be the best person that each one could possibly be.

Lataya is a graduate of Texas Southern University where she earned a degree in Journalism. In addition to being a writer, Lataya is a speaker, presentation coach, wife and mom.

For more information on booking this author to speak at your event or to conduct a book signing, visit www.allaboutspeakers.com or www.latayasimpson.com.

LET'S GET SOCIAL!

Connect with me on my blog: Being More Than Pretty, Facebook, Twitter, and Pinterest!

www.latayasimpson.com – BLOG:

BLOGGING WITH LATAYA SIMPSON, AUTHOR OF MORE THAN PRETTY

Facebook.com/AuthorLatayaSimpson

Twitter.com/LatayaSimpson

Pinterest.com/latayasimpson

COMING IN 2014

This 10-week spiritual enrichment study takes a look at the deeper meaning behind the question, "Why me?" The study is designed to help readers improve coping skills.

Recommended for small group bible study, book clubs and support groups.

COMING IN 2014

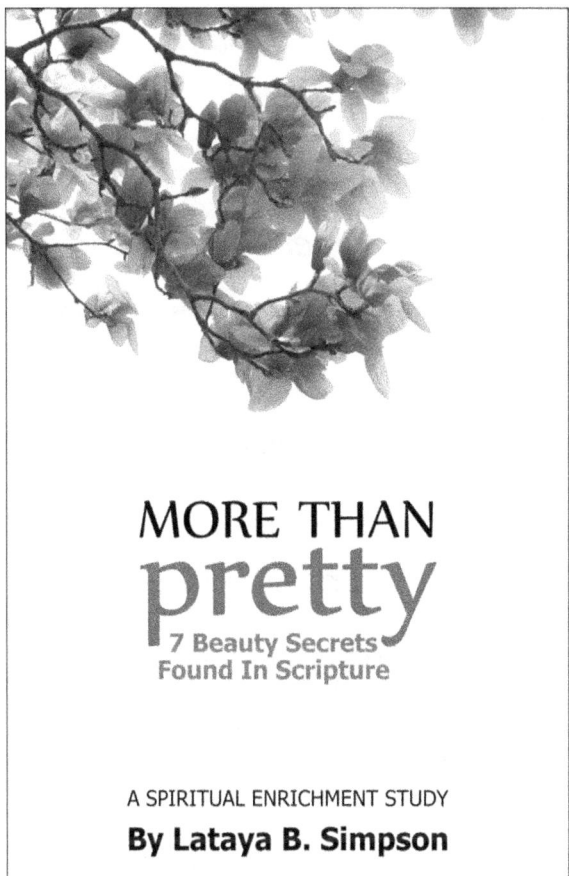

More Than Pretty: 7 Beauty Secrets Found in Scripture
is a companion Bible study for women and teens.
Visit our web site for more information!

Host a Book Show

If you're in the Houston area you're invited to consider hosting a book show! A More Than Pretty book show is like a mini retreat in your own home! Invite your friends and family for games, prizes, inspiration and story sharing.

Guests will be able to purchase an autographed copy of the book at a discounted price in addition to items such as gift sets and spa sets.

Visit www.latayasimpson.com for more information on signing up!

www.ingramcontent.com/pod-product-compliance
Lightning Source LLC
Chambersburg PA
CBHW071134090426
42736CB00012B/2116